I0794470

ACTS OF THE APOSTLES

THE FIFTH GOSPEL

STREAMS of MERCY
study series

Gary Holloway

Acts of the Apostles:
The Fifth Gospel

LEAFWOOD
PUBLISHERS

1648 Campus Ct.
Abilene, TX 79601
www.leafwoodpublishers.com

Cover Design by Mark Decker

Printed in the United States of America

ISBN 0-89112-239-7

2 3 4 5

Table of Contents

FOR TEACHERS AND CLASS LEADERS

The Word of God is powerful. This belief is the driving force behind the Streams of Mercy Study Series. Assigned reading, brief commentary, and questions for reflection and class discussion are presented for each section of the biblical book. The goal is changed lives—changed by the power of the Word.

Consider the following suggestions as you prepare for class:

- Even though class members may have read the passage assigned for the week, select some verses to be read aloud in class: let the Word speak.
- Give a brief summary of the points made in the lesson; then begin working with the questions. As you prepare for your class, explore the possibility of a variety of answers to the questions. Don't be afraid of momentary silence when you ask the questions; give people a chance to think, but be prepared to prompt the discussion.
- Be creative with your classroom time. Sometimes have the class work in small groups to discuss the questions. Consider having someone prepare to comment on a particular question for the next scheduled class meeting. Perhaps you could ask someone to share his or her experience concerning balancing time to work on lessons in the middle of work and family obligations—in this way you acknowledge the struggle to fit in Bible study. Give someone the task of praying, throughout the coming week, for the whole class as they all find time for study. Let the class know these prayers will be offered on their behalf.
- Ask class members to make a plan of action that puts into practice matters the text addresses. This practical plan may include a service project or a commitment to pray for help in overcoming specific problems the text brings to light. Be prepared to suggest plans of action and to get the class involved in brainstorming. Avoid taking charge too much; let the class get involved.
- Find out if anyone in the class would like to create banners or any kind of visuals pertaining to the study. This is a good way to validate the gifts of others.
- Try to inspire excitement about the class working together each week to hear and understand the Word of God. Stress that this is one of the ways we are in fellowship with one another.

- Be sensitive to people who don't want to speak in class. Encourage those who want to speak, but who may be a little tentative. Practice good leadership by not allowing any one person to dominate the discussions.

- Try to keep the discussions on target. One complaint we often hear about Bible classes is that the group gets off the subject too easily. These volumes are designed to promote healthy discussion of the biblical text. Pray for help to keep the class focused.

- To remind us of the active Jesus we follow, each chapter of this study guide will open with a "Jesus Alive!" section, showing how that part of Acts tells the ongoing story of Jesus.

Nothing is more important than seeking God's guidance as you prepare for class. Ask him to open your heart so the text speaks to you and convicts you; then you will be more prepared to lead the group. May the Lord bless all of you as you seek his will, and may you know the everflowing streams of his mercy.

INTRODUCTION

"If only we could have been there to see Jesus in the flesh." Many of us have had that same thought, perhaps believing that Jesus left his disciples alone after his ascension. Since then, he has been away from his followers, until he comes again.

Nothing could be further from the truth. Jesus never abandoned his disciples. Even after his return to the Father, he lives *in* them, empowering them for service through the Holy Spirit. His body, the church, is still on earth. Jesus thus still teaches, heals, and tells good news through those of us who follow him.

To put it differently, our experience of Jesus is not less than that of the disciples who saw him in the flesh. In some ways, we even have an advantage over them, in that his promise of the Holy Spirit comes to fruition only after his ascension. We should never think of Jesus as far removed from us. Jesus is alive and well on planet Earth. The gospel is not just an old story from long ago; it is a living gospel of a living Lord.

Perhaps the arrangement of our Bibles gives us the false impression that Jesus left his disciples to follow his example on our own. At one level, it certainly makes sense to place the four gospels—Matthew, Mark, Luke, and John—together at the beginning of the New Testament. John is last because it is different from the others. However, this arrangement split Luke's gospel in two. Luke writes a first volume and then a second one (see Acts 1:1), all on the subject of what Jesus did. Volume one, Luke, tells what Jesus did "until the day he was taken up to heaven," and the second volume, Acts, tells what Jesus continued to do through the Holy Spirit among his disciples.

Luke goes to great pains to show that what Jesus does in his physical body in the Gospel of Luke, he continues to do in his spiritual body, the church, in Acts. Notice the following parallels:

LUKE	ACTS
Jesus receives the Spirit, then begins his ministry (3:22).	Apostles receive the Spirit, then begin to witness (2:4).
Jesus heals at the roadside (18:35-43).	Peter and John heal at the Temple gate (3:1-10).
Jesus is rejected in his hometown—Nazareth (4:14-30).	The church is rejected in its "hometown"—Jerusalem (8:1).
Jesus heals a paralytic, saying "Take up your mat..." (5:17-26).	Peter heals a paralytic with the same words (9:32-35).
Jesus raises Jairus' daughter (8:49-56).	Peter raises Dorcas (9:40-41).
Jesus heals by the hem of his garment (8:42-48).	Peter heals with his shadow (5:15); Paul with his handkerchiefs (19:11).

Acts is more than the apostles and the early church doing what Jesus did; it is the story of Jesus still at work among them. For example, Peter, John, Paul and others always heal "in the name of Jesus" in the book of Acts. To heal in his name means Jesus is still at work in the world, empowering his disciples for service through the Holy Spirit.

Acts thus is best thought of as a fifth Gospel, an idea that has significant implications for how we understand Acts and how we view our own discipleship. Jesus did not abandon his disciples at the ascension, but continued to live in them though his Holy Spirit. In the same way, Jesus lives in his disciples today. Thus, the book of Acts is more than a record of what the church did long ago. Instead, we can read it as a living account of what Jesus is still doing in his church. In Jesus' own words: "But you will receive power when the Holy Spirit comes on you; and you will be my witnesses in Jerusalem, and in all Judea and Samaria, and to the ends of the earth" (Acts 1:11). As we read Acts, we will see the power of their witness in the face of great opposition. As we read, we also should see the work of Jesus in our lives today. We too are empowered to be witnesses. And no opposition—not persecution, hypocrisy, nor powerful rulers—can stand against that Spirit-filled witness.

Acts is best thought of as a fifth Gospel.

1

Gospel Witness

Acts 1:1-26

Jesus Alive!

This first chapter of Acts makes it clear that Jesus is alive. The disciples see him in the flesh! Jesus speaks his last words and ascends into heaven; yet, as we shall see in the rest of Acts, these are not the last words or the last acts of Jesus. He still lives, speaks, and acts in his followers through his Holy Spirit.

Waiting for the Gift (Acts 1:1-5)

Practice what you preach. As one who preaches and teaches, I try to take that advice to heart. However, if we look at the life of Jesus, we find the relation between action and teaching more dynamic than simply putting actions to words. To Jesus, the gospel was more than something he taught; it was what he embodied. Luke summarizes his gospel as what Jesus both began to *teach* and to *do*. One sees the pattern clearly in Luke. Jesus heals and then uses the healing as an opportunity to teach. He teaches and feeds a multitude. He sometimes even stops his teaching and leaves his students behind in order to pray by himself.

> *Luke summarizes his gospel as what Jesus both began to* teach *and to* do.

Jesus commends this same rhythm of action and witness to his disciples. Strangely, the first "action" he calls them to is to *wait*. If there is one thing I cannot stand, it's waiting. I'm one of those who jump from line to line in the supermarket, hoping to check out quickly. Instead, it seems that whatever line I am in is the slowest.

We do not want to wait. We want to be active disciples, up and doing for our Lord. But Jesus tells his disciples to wait for a gift from God, the promised Holy Spirit. Only by that power can they be effective witnesses to the good news of Jesus.

Reflection and Application

1. How would you briefly summarize the life of Jesus?

2. Does "waiting" sound too passive for dedicated Christians? Shouldn't we be out there "doing" things for Jesus, instead of merely waiting? Why did Jesus tell these disciples to wait?

You Will Be My Witnesses (Acts 1:6-11)

"What time is it?" An innocent question, but one we ask often, and not just about the time of day. Many Christians want to know God's timetable for their lives. Is it time to wait? To be active? Time for caution? For boldness? Others try to read the "signs of the times" in the Middle East or in terrorist acts at home to determine when Jesus will return.

The disciples are no different. They want to know if now is the time for the kingdom. Jesus points them (and us) away from knowledge about the time toward the service he wants them to perform. "You will be my witnesses." God will work in his own time and ways to bring in the kingdom. Our task is to witness to what he has done through the death and resurrection of Jesus. That witness may take us across the street or across the globe. Through that mission of proclaiming the good news of Jesus, God will reign in human hearts and the kingdom will come.

But strength for the task of witnessing does not come from us alone. It comes from the power of the Spirit. Perhaps the contemporary church has failed to be the witness Jesus desires us to be because we trust our own power. True witness is always in the power of the Spirit.

After Jesus commissions his disciples as witnesses, he ascends and disappears from their sight. Is Jesus abandoning his disciples? Of course not! Like Elisha, who was promised a double portion of the spirit of Elijah if he saw him ascend (1 Kings 9-10), the disciples receive the Holy Spirit only after the ascension of Jesus. The Spirit does not take the place of Jesus, but rather Jesus continues to be with his disciples through the Spirit.

Jesus did not abandon his disciples. He will not abandon us. He is still with us through his Holy Spirit. What's more, we have the testimony of angels that he will return. Now we live between ascension and Second Coming as witnesses through the Spirit's power.

Reflection and Application

1. Do we worry sometimes about God's timetable for our lives and for the world? What does this passage say about those worries?

2. Does the ascension of Jesus make you feel he has left us? Should we feel that way?

The Twelve (Acts 1:12-26)

Numbers are important. Kids get upset if we forget their ages, wives and husbands if we forget the date of our anniversary. In the Bible, certain numbers are particularly important like three, seven, and twelve.

The twelve. Why was it so important to have twelve apostles? Wouldn't eleven do? Yes, if twelve were just any old number. But the twelve apostles stood for the twelve tribes of Israel. God was restoring Israel through the witness of the twelve apostles.

Thus, the defection of Judas left a gap that had to be filled. Notice how Peter doesn't let Judas off the hook for his actions. Instead, he calls them wickedness. Yet, Peter assures us that the betrayal by Judas *does not destroy the plan of God.* Through David in the Psalms, God spoke of this one whose place would be taken by another (Psalm 69:25). Human action is free; Judas chose to be a traitor, but human action cannot thwart the purposes of God.

So another leader must be chosen—but how? First, there is a description of the type of leader needed. He must be one who accompanied Jesus from John's baptism to the ascension. Two men, Joseph and Matthias, meet the description. But only one apostle is needed to bring the number to twelve. How to choose between them?

Jesus makes the choice through a praying church. About a hundred and twenty believers gather, constantly in prayer. They do not make this important decision by majority vote, but through prayer allow Jesus to choose this apostle as he chose the original twelve. How does Jesus make his decision known? Through the casting of lots. We're not sure exactly how that worked—perhaps they drew straws, put names in a hat, or wrote names on stones that were thrown or cast. However, this was not a game of chance, but the way the Lord Jesus answered their prayer for guidance.

Should we cast lots today? Some Christians do. If we decide to, we must let the decision come from the Lord. More importantly, Jesus should guide every major decision we make through prayer. Interestingly, this is the last mention of casting lots in Acts. Perhaps after the Spirit comes at Pentecost, it is through his indwelling that the disciples get an answer to their prayers for guidance.

Again, the main point is that Jesus has not abandoned his followers. He still works with chosen leaders who will serve as witnesses to the good news.

Reflection and Application

1. If Judas fulfilled scripture by his betrayal, then was he completely responsible for his actions? How do we balance biblical teaching on personal responsibility with biblical teaching on the sovereign plans of God?

2. How should we choose leaders today? What is the place of prayer? Of casting lots?

A Closer Look

1. Why have some been reluctant to call contemporary Christians "witnesses?" Are those who "witness" to others about Jesus today the same kind of witnesses the apostles were? What does it mean to "witness?"

2. In what way was Jesus restoring Israel? Are Christians today part of a restored Israel? If so, what does this imply for how Christians treat Jews?

2

A Church of Signs and Wonders

Acts 2:1-47

Jesus Alive!

We usually think of Pentecost as the birth of the church. In a way, it was the church's beginning, but there were disciples (and therefore in some sense, a church) before Pentecost. It might be better to see Pentecost as the day Jesus comes to live in his church in a new way. No longer will he be with his disciples in the flesh, but he will powerfully be in them through the Holy Spirit. All the wonders they do in his name show his continuing life in his body, the church.

The Coming of the Spirit (Acts 2:1-13)

Wind. Fire. Speaking in tongues. Could there be a more exciting day than Pentecost? The events of this chapter reflect several earlier Bible stories. Some think Pentecost celebrated the giving of God's instruction at Sinai (also accompanied with loud sounds and fire, Exod 19:16-19). Now God gives his instruction through the Spirit and the apostles. Others see in the speaking in tongues a great reversal of the curse of Babel (Gen 11:1-9). Humanity, divided at Babel, now unites in Christ.

Whatever the background, Pentecost is a formative day for the church. The promise of Jesus to send the Spirit dramatically comes to fulfillment. Just as with the earthly ministry of Jesus, the coming of the Spirit divides people into two camps. Some accept wind, fire, and tongues as signs from God, signs that need explaining. Others, out of unbelief, ridicule what they hear as drunken ramblings. Later in Acts, we will see the same variety of responses when the Spirit comes.

Reflection and Application

1. How do you picture the coming of the Spirit to and on the apostles? How does the scene change from an upper room to where a large crowd can gather?

2. What exactly is speaking in tongues? What is the purpose of tongues here? Why did some understand and others not understand the tongues? If we have the Spirit, shouldn't we speak in tongues today?

The Sermon (Acts 2:14-36)

As exciting as the wind, fire, and speaking in tongues were, the sermon at Pentecost marked the climax.

Disappointed? Perhaps yes, because contemporary people see sermons and speeches as boring. They are only words and talk is cheap. But think of the power of great speeches in history: Abraham Lincoln's Gettysburg Address rallies a nation in time of war; Martin Luther King's "I Have a Dream" speech leads to the liberation of a people. Words can and do have power!

And these words at Pentecost are not mere human words. Peter's talk is not cheap; it is the story of the gospel, the good news that cost Jesus his life. Peter outlines the life of Jesus, including his death and resurrection. This is the greatest story ever told—the old, old story of Jesus and his love. But it was a new story to these listeners, especially the part about resurrection. Why should the crowd believe Peter?

He convinces them from Scripture, quoting David in the Psalms. He tells them that he and the disciples are eyewitnesses of the resurrected Jesus. His "clincher" argument is that Jesus has poured forth what they have seen and heard that day. They may doubt Peter, but they cannot easily doubt what they hear with their own ears. Those speaking in tongues say this amazing ability comes from Jesus. If he can send tongues, he must be alive; if alive, he is no blasphemer and charlatan. He *is* what he claimed to be—Lord and Christ. And this crowd has killed their long-awaited Messiah.

How in the world can they make that right?

Reflection and Application

1. Do we still feel the power of Peter's sermon, or has the story become too old to us? What can we do to recover the power of the gospel story in our lives?

2. Why did Peter even make an argument from Scripture in the sermon? Weren't the tongues enough? What is the point of the Psalms passages?

The Response (Acts 2:37-41)

Those convinced of the resurrection of the Messiah they had killed now realize the enormity of their guilt. No wonder they cry out, "Brothers, what shall we do?" It is a cry of desperation. How could God forgive those who killed the ultimate prophet?

However, it is forgiveness that Peter promises, forgiveness through the name of this Jesus, the one they killed. Peter calls for a complete change of mind, heart, and life. Jesus is not who they thought he was. He is not blasphemer but Lord. From hatred of Jesus, they must turn to love and obedience.

This radical change of life is symbolized in baptism in the name of Jesus. Baptism is no empty ritual but a dynamic experience of discipleship, cleansing, and reception of the Holy Spirit. Joel's promise that the Spirit would be poured out on all people comes true for these listeners and even for those "far off" (including us). With such a great promise of salvation, no wonder about three thousand respond that day, experience baptism, and are added to the number of the disciples.

Reflection and Application

1. How did the crowd feel when they were convinced they had killed the Messiah? Can we identify with the depth of their guilt? Was the gospel story better news to them than to us?

2. What is the connection between repentance and baptism? Among baptism, forgiveness, and the gift of the Holy Spirit? Should we separate any of these three from the other?

From Excitement to Devotion (Acts 2:42-47)

On Pentecost, the sound of a tornado fills the room, tongues of fire appear, the Holy Spirit fills some of the disciples, and they speak in other tongues. On that day, Peter tells the crowd of Jesus, one "...accredited by God to you by miracles, wonders, and signs" (Acts 2:22). Peter calls them to faith in Jesus. Three thousand respond and are baptized. The church begins with miracles.

How did these first Christians respond to the miracles? Luke says they responded with devotion. Miracles caused excitement and enthusiasm. The early church transformed that momentary enthusiasm into permanent devotion. To be devoted to something means to make it a constant practice. It implies dedication, discipline, and habit. The Jerusalem Christians experienced the thrill of miracle—but they wanted more. From them, we learn to devote ourselves to a life of discipleship—a life of *more.*

They wanted to learn *more* of this Jesus they now followed, so they listened to the apostle's teaching. They shared *more* than they ever had before—a common faith, life, food, and even money. They prayed together often in the name of Jesus. They worshipped God through Christ in joy. Because of their witness, they grew *more.* They grew not because they had discovered some evangelism technique, but because they told the good news of Jesus. They told it plainly and boldly, and Lord Jesus gave the increase.

If we are to experience the power of Pentecost, we too must turn our momentary excitement into permanent devotion to Jesus.

Reflection and Application

1. According to Acts 2:42, these first Christians devoted themselves to four things. What are the four, and which one do we lack the most today? Why? What can we do to gain more devotion to it?

2. Should Christians share their possessions with each other? When? How? Does this mean there should be no private property?

A Closer Look

1. Are you a "Pentecostal?" What does that term usually mean? Shouldn't *all* Christians be Pentecostal? How do the events of Pentecost mold the church today?

2. Note what Jesus does in this chapter. He sends the Spirit (Acts 2:33, 38). He forgives sins through baptism (Acts 2:38). He adds to the number of the disciples (Acts 2:47). Do we think he is as active today as he was on Pentecost?

3

The Gospel Under Fire

Acts 3:1-4:31

Jesus Alive!

In this section, Peter calls Jesus "the author of life" (Acts 3:15). Jesus acts as the source of life through his own resurrection, but also by his power to bring healing and new life. Peter and John heal in the name of Jesus. The disciples boldly proclaim the good news of Jesus. For the first time they face what Jesus faced, threats and persecution. Moreover, they rely on the power of the living Jesus to remove their fears and make them bold witnesses.

Jesus Still Heals (Acts 3:1-10)

They sit by the sidewalk and beg. If you work downtown in a large city, you see them. What do we do? Fear them? Ignore them? Give them money, but wonder if that is really what they need? Do we give only to those who are obviously ill or disabled?

> *Disciples rely on the power of the living Jesusto remove their fears and make them bold witnesses.*

The same questions must have occurred to Peter and John as they met the crippled man at the gate of the temple area. He obviously wanted money. Peter said, "We don't have any." That itself is interesting. Three thousand disciples share their money with one another, but Peter and the rest of the apostles have no money. They certainly did not get rich off the gospel.

But Peter and John have far more than money; they have the power of Jesus: "In the name of Jesus, walk," they command. And the lame man walks, jumps, and praises. Where did they learn to treat those in need this way? From Jesus, who saw a blind man at a gate and gave him his sight (Luke 18:35-43). From Jesus, who gave compassion and power. Indeed, as they make clear, it is not Peter and John healing, but *Jesus himself* who makes the man walk. "In the name of Jesus" is not an empty phrase—it is Luke's way of reminding us that Jesus is alive and active in his disciples.

Reflection and Application

1. How would Jesus treat those today who beg by the side of the road? Would he give them money? Would he do more than that?

2. Do we still tend to put the work of Jesus completely in the past? Did his ministry end with the ascension? Does Jesus still minister today? How?

The Sermon (Acts 3:11-26)

When the crippled man, now healed, starts leaping and shouting praise, he draws a crowd. Peter takes the opportunity to explain the origin of the miracle. In a sense, there is only one sermon in Acts. Whether Peter at Pentecost or after this miracle, or Paul and others in the synagogues and marketplaces, the sermon *always* centers on Christ. A gospel sermon is the telling of the good news of Jesus.

Peter points the crowd away from their interest in John and him. The glorified Jesus healed this man. If he can heal, then he is alive, risen from the dead. This Jerusalem crowd had "killed the author of life," but if they repent and turn to Jesus, their sins will be wiped out. Jesus has been sent to them, through the apostles, to turn each of them from their wicked ways.

Repent! Turn! That is the essence of Peter's message to them and to us. Turning may seem like a human action. If we simply quit our wickedness, then God will forgive. But note that this turning is more than a human action. It is in response to the resurrected Jesus. He is the one who moves us to turn to him. He is the one who refreshes. He wipes the slate clean. He comes to restore all things. The Jesus who has the power to heal this lame man is the same Jesus who has the power to heal our wickedness today and for all time.

Reflection and Application

1. What makes for a "gospel sermon?" Is every religious lesson a gospel message? Should each one be?

2. What picture of salvation in this section means the most to you? Sins wiped out? All things restored? Times of refreshing? Why?

Strong Reactions (Acts 4:1-22)

Peter's sermon may not startle us—we have heard it all before—but it called forth extreme reactions in that day. Many in the crowd responded to the good news in faith. The number of believers reached about five thousand. What phenomenal growth! The gospel is indeed powerful.

Yet, the gospel also calls forth powerful opposition. The same forces who led to the death of Jesus—priests, temple guards, and Sadducees—arrest Peter and John and toss them in jail overnight. The next day, these powerful rulers ask them at trial to explain their power and authority for healing the crippled man.

Peter answers boldly and clearly. "It is by the name of Jesus of Nazareth, whom you crucified but whom God raised from the dead, that this man stands before you healed?" (Acts 4:10). Peter's boldness startles these leaders. They can see he and John have been with Jesus and share his courage. The rulers are at a complete loss. They want to silence these men who accuse them of killing the Messiah, but they can't easily prosecute them for an act of kindness to a lame man.

Peter and John reply confidently to the threats of these leaders. "We cannot help speaking about what we have seen and heard" (Acts 4:20). This same Peter denied Jesus three times because he feared for his safety. Now that fear is gone, washed away in the reality of what he had seen and heard, the reality of a living Lord Jesus and a poured-out Spirit.

Reflection and Application

1. Why is it so few Americans react strongly to the gospel today? Is lack of opposition to Christianity an "unmixed" blessing?

2. Do we find it easy to be silent about what we have seen and heard about Jesus? What does it take to keep us silent? Would threats from authorities make us less or more bold in our faith?

A Prayer for Boldness (Acts 4:23-31)

Having boldly proclaimed Jesus in the face of threats, the disciples do not congratulate themselves. Perhaps they know that next time they might succumb to persecution and keep silent about their Lord. Instead of relying on their own courage, they bring their weakness to God in prayer.

And they are honest in prayer. They do not put an optimistic spin on their situation. The powerful forces against them—nations and kings, Herod and Pilate, and Gentiles and Jewish leaders—are the same forces arrayed against Jesus himself. Yet, they also confess that no human power can stand against the will of almighty God.

They do not pray that God will leave them alone in comfort and safety. Instead, they pray that more healings, signs, and wonders will take place in the name of Jesus. It was healing that got them in trouble, but they do not back away from the trouble; instead, they pray for boldness from God.

And God answers! The house shakes, the Spirit fills them, and they do speak with boldness. Today's church needs to be shaken. Today's church needs boldness. We face little persecution for our faith, yet our Christian witness is tentative and apologetic. We believe in Christ, but we don't want to "force that belief on others." Many Christians have bought into our culture's teaching that one faith is as good as another. We have abandoned, or at least apologize for the exclusiveness of Christianity: that no other name but Jesus can save. We need courage to speak what we have seen and heard, to proclaim the good news of Jesus. We need the courage that comes only through prayer.

Reflection and Application

1. What would our prayer be in a similar situation? If imprisoned and commanded to speak no more of Jesus, would we pray for safety? Would we ask God to change the hearts of the officials? Would we ask for persecution to cease?

2. Do we need boldness in our faith today? How can we get it?

A Closer Look

1. Do we face any opposition to Christianity today? What form does that opposition take? Is our situation worse or better than that of the apostles?

2. God immediately answers the prayer of these disciples. Why doesn't he always answer this soon or this dramatically? Do they (and we) sometimes have to wait for an answer? How do we wait?

4

THREATS TO THE GOSPEL

ACTS 4:32-8:1

Jesus Alive!

If Jesus is alive, then our discipleship must also be living and not false. The living Jesus does not require perfect disciples, but he does want sincere ones. He motivates that sincerity by severely punishing those who think they can fool his Spirit. The living Jesus protects and encourages his disciples when they face opposition. The living Jesus cares for all needy disciples, and wants to unite them all. A risen Lord ably handles threats to his body, the church.

The Threat of Hypocrisy (Acts 4:32-5:11)

The power of the gospel changed the lives of the early disciples. It even changed their spending habits; because of their common life in Christ, these believers even shared their possessions. Some, like Barnabas, even sold their real estate investments to help those in need.

But the power of the gospel can be corrupted. Remember that Ananias and Sapphira also sold property to give to the poor; however, they kept part of the proceeds for themselves. That in itself was not wrong. How many of us have given even *part* of our investments to feed the poor? The problem, in this case, is they lie and claim they are giving it all to others.

Why? Why did they lie to the church and especially to the Holy Spirit? Because they wanted others to think they were as generous as Barnabas. They wanted to look better than they really were. We call it hypocrisy. God struck them dead for it. Why such harsh punishment? Will God forgive hypocrisy? I sure hope so! Haven't we all at times wanted to look more spiritual than we actually are? Nevertheless, what if God had let Ananias and Sapphira off lightly? Wouldn't that have sent the message that discipleship was something one could fake? Christianity could be played at instead of being taken seriously.

> *We are more afraid of what others think of us than we are of offending the Holy God.*

"Great fear seized the whole church and all who heard about these events" (Acts 5:11). I guess so! We must fear a God who will strike us dead if we try to fool him. There is a place for such fear of God. Perhaps our churches today are weak because we fear the wrong thing. We are more afraid of what others think of us than we are of offending the Holy God.

Reflection and Application

1. What might have happened if Ananias and Sapphira had gotten away with their hypocrisy? Could hypocritical Christians have destroyed the church?

2. What kind of threat is hypocrisy to the church today? What can be done to face that threat?

The Threat of Persecution (Acts 5:12-42)

In addition to the internal threat of hypocrisy, the church continued to face the external pressure of persecution. The amazing power of Jesus through the apostles (Peter could even heal with his shadow) marked them as the true leaders of Israel. The high priest and his associates thought they were in control and jailed the apostles, out of jealousy.

However, the angel of the Lord (in this context, I believe it is the angel of the Lord Jesus) releases them and tells them to proclaim boldly the message in the temple courts. The Sanhedrin sends to the jail for them, finds they have disappeared, and is shocked to learn the apostles are doing exactly what they had been forbidden to do. They proclaimed the resurrected Jesus.

The Sanhedrin politely requests the apostles to appear before them. Their politeness soon turns to threats. The apostles boldly reply, "We must obey God rather than men!" (Acts 5:29). The infuriated Sanhedrin then wants to kill them. They are stopped by the wise advice of Gamaliel.

The real question in this section is "Who is in charge?" The Sanhedrin thinks they have the power to stop the gospel; instead, the resurrected Jesus has given power to the apostles as the true leaders of Israel. We may think that the government or our boss or public opinion have the power to make us be quiet about the good news of Jesus. We, like these apostles, can be bold in our proclamation if we see who really is in charge. It is God, not human authority, which we must obey.

Reflection and Application

1. Name some ways our government makes us afraid to proclaim the gospel boldly. What forces in our workplaces make us less bold in our faith than we ought to be?

2. Is Gamaliel's advice (Acts 5:34-39) relevant to us today? Should we leave certain religious teachers alone to see if their teaching is from God or merely human?

The Threat of Disunity (Acts 6:1-7)

Some thought the church was neglecting certain widows. This neglect seems like such a small problem compared to persecution. However, in my experience, most church splits occur not because of outside pressure or doctrinal differences, but because certain groups feel neglected. Similarly, the "widow problem" reflected a difference in language and culture, Grecian Jews versus Hebraic Jews in the church. How many times have our church splits been over differences in race, culture, age, and outlook? How many times have people left because they felt the church ignored their group's viewpoint?

This threat to the unity of the church is serious. The apostles respond by asking the church to choose seven leaders to care for these widows. Note that waiting tables is not beneath the dignity of the apostles. Jesus had taught them to wash others' feet (John 13:1-20). Caring for those in need is the heart of the gospel. But the apostles knew the story of Jesus better than others. They should devote themselves to prayer and the ministry of the word.

Of the seven who are chosen to care for the widows, two later become bold proclaimers of the gospel—Stephen and Philip. "Benevolence" ministries and "evangelism" ministries always go together. Through prayer and the laying on of hands, these seven receive the power of Jesus to serve and to proclaim the gospel boldly. Consequently widows are served, the church is unified, the gospel is preached, and the number of disciples increases.

Reflection and Application

1. What groups in your church are being neglected? What can be done to help them? What places do leadership, service, and prayer play in that help?

2. What is the relationship between benevolence and evangelism? Have we separated those ministries in our churches? Should we?

The Threat of Death (Acts 6:8-8:1)

The persecution the apostles faced intensifies. Because of his bold preaching and great wonders, Stephen is put on trial before the Sanhedrin. Stephen's long defense before them may look like nothing more to us than a history lesson. Yet, at the end of his speech, the Sanhedrin is furious. What makes them so mad?

If we examine the speech closely, we find that the sacred history Stephen recounts is a challenge to the exclusiveness and the authority of the Jewish leaders. Stephen makes it clear that God works outside of the borders of Israel: he calls Abraham in Mesopotamia (Acts 7:2); he blesses Joseph in Egypt (Acts 7:10); he is with Moses in Egypt and at Sinai (Acts 7:20-38). Stephen also makes it clear that their ancestors rejected obedience to God, rebelled against Moses, and killed the prophets (Acts 7:39-50). Finally, when God sent them his Son as the ultimate prophet, this very Sanhedrin condemned him to death (Acts 7:51-53).

The Sanhedrin knows their guilt, but instead of reacting with repentance, they kill the messenger. They drag Stephen outside the city and stone him to death.

What is striking about this section are the similarities between Stephen and Jesus. Like Jesus, Stephen shows grace, power, and wisdom, through the Holy Spirit. He faces the same false accusation Jesus faced—that he spoke against the holy temple. Like Jesus, Stephen is confronted by false witnesses. He is executed outside the city, asks for forgiveness for his killers, prays that his spirit be received, and is buried by godly people. In all these ways, his death parallels the death of Jesus.

There is one significant difference. Jesus, unlike Stephen, died for the sins of the world. However, when Jesus told his followers to take up the cross daily and follow him (Luke 9:23), he knew that some would have to fulfill that command literally. The Jesus who died on the cross is the resurrected Jesus who also dies in the person of his disciple, Stephen.

Stephen gives the last full measure of devotion to his Lord Jesus. This death could have been the end of the gospel and the church. How many are willing to face death for Jesus? How can the church stand this persecution? Can the Jewish leaders who could not stop Jesus now stop his followers?

> *The power of Jesus through the gospel can overcome any obstacle.*

But the power of Jesus through the gospel can overcome any obstacle. This is not the end of the church; it is a new beginning. Through the death of Stephen, a new era will open in the story of the spread of the good news.

Reflection and Application

1. Would you be willing to die for Jesus? Are we willing to face lesser forms of persecution for him?

2. Is there a time to make people angry because we tell them the gospel? Would Stephen have been more effective if he had told the Sanhedrin more of what they wanted to hear?

A Closer Look

1. What most threatens the church today? Are the threats in this chapter still around? What can we do to overcome these threats?

2. Is Jesus less powerful in our churches than he was in the early church? Does he show his power in the same way?

5

God's Suprising Plan

Acts 8:2-9:31

Jesus Alive!

Things are not always how they appear in the life of Jesus. We don't expect a King in a manger or God in a carpenter's shop. What looks like the greatest defeat of all—dying like a criminal on a cross—turns to victory in the resurrection. In Acts, Jesus continues to turn the greatest defeats, even the death of one of his followers, into victories for the good news.

The Defeat of the Gospel? (Acts 8:1-3)

Stephen's death looks like the beginning of the end for the church. If preaching the good news of Jesus results in death, then who will spread the gospel? A united church, sharing in all things, now is divided and scattered. A church that relied on the apostles to teach and guide is now without that leadership. A church that prayed for boldness now runs away to escape persecution.

Is this the end of the church? Saul certainly hopes so. He is not content to kill those who, like Stephen, boldly proclaim the message publicly. Instead, he goes into their homes, perhaps their house church meetings, and drags them off to jail. How can the church survive?

One even wonders about the actions of the apostles during this persecution. Do they remain in Jerusalem to show they are unafraid of persecution? Or are the authorities afraid to persecute them because of the power of Jesus in them? Jesus had told the apostles that they would be his witnesses in Jerusalem, Judea, Samaria, and the world. Why does it take them so long to leave Jerusalem and witness? How can the gospel survive without the apostles traveling and spreading the news?

Reflection and Application

1. What would happen to your congregation if the authorities came in and dragged many off to jail for their faith? Would this hurt or help the church?

2. Why do the apostles stay in Jerusalem? Is it deep faith or lack of trust that makes them stay?

Good News to Samaria (Acts 8:4-17)

The Lord Jesus turns defeat into victory. The scattering of the church due to persecution is not the end of the gospel but actually spreads it. For example, Philip, one of the seven chosen to care for the widows, proclaims Christ in Samaria. The power of Jesus, through Philip, cures the sick and casts out demons in Samaria.

> *No force, human or supernatural, can stand against the power of Christ through the gospel.*

Consequently, many believe, including a magician named Simon who formerly had amazed the Samaritans. When Simon saw the genuine miracles of Philip, he also is baptized. In Jerusalem the question had been, "Who has power, the Sanhedrin or Jesus through the apostles?" Here the question is "Who has the power, Simon the follower of the Great Power, or Philip, the follower of Jesus?" No force, human or supernatural, can stand against the power of Christ through the gospel.

A puzzling aspect of this episode is the relationship of baptism and the reception of the Holy Spirit. At Pentecost, the gift of the Spirit is promised at baptism (Acts 2:38). Here, the Samaritans are baptized but do not receive the Spirit until Peter and John lay hands on them. Why the difference? We are not told directly in the story, but it might have something to do with the need for the apostles to validate the Samaritan mission. The work of Philip was not to begin a new church, completely separate from that in Jerusalem; instead, through the persons of Peter and John, the Jerusalem church shows its oneness with these Samaritan believers.

Reflection and Application

1. Do some people today claim to have supernatural power? Are there evil supernatural forces that claim authority over us? If so, what should our attitude be toward them?

2. In what sense was the Samaritan church separate from the Jerusalem church? How were they one church? What should be the relationship among congregations of the Lord's church today? Are they one or separate?

Controlling the Spirit (Acts 8:18-25)

How does the Spirit work in the Book of Acts? Two answers. One, he works in different ways. Two, he works any way he wants. We must be careful, lest we think we have the Spirit figured out. We do not control him. We hope he controls us.

Simon makes the mistake of thinking he can control the Spirit of God, perhaps as he controlled whatever power enabled him to practice sorcery. Seeing that the Spirit came through the laying on of hands, he errs by thinking Peter and John could control the Spirit. He offers to buy that control.

Peter's response is frightening. He tells Simon to repent and pray, then *perhaps* God will forgive him. That is a scary "perhaps." Peter knows the heart of God, that he wants all to repent. However, it is a fearful thing to try to manipulate the Spirit of God. This manipulation of the Spirit comes close to what Jesus described as the unpardonable sin (Mark 3:29). Simon is correctly frightened enough to ask Peter to pray for him.

Can we commit the sin of Simon today? At first glance, it may seem unlikely. We are not about to try to buy the power of the Spirit. But don't we sometimes think we can manipulate God? Don't some Christians today think they can buy influence with money? Do we not all, at times, try to bargain with God? Perhaps Simon is not the only one who needs to repent.

Reflection and Application

1. What similarities are there between the sin of Simon and the sin of Ananias and Sapphira? Can we lie to the Holy Spirit or try to buy him today?

2. Name some ways we try to control God. What would it look like if we repented of those attempts?

The Gospel for All (Acts 8:26-40)

Jesus works in mysterious ways to spread the gospel in the Book of Acts. He takes evil acts, the death of Stephen, and the persecution of the church, using them to scatter his followers to preach the word. Here he takes a preacher from a successful ministry and sends him to a desert road. Yet by this action, the gospel spreads to a new part of the world.

The prophets had spoken of "eunuchs who keep my sabbaths" receiving blessings from God (Isaiah 56:4-5), and of God reclaiming a remnant from Ethiopia or Cush (Isaiah 11:11). Here an Ethiopian eunuch, perhaps a God-fearing Gentile or a convert to Judaism, comes to faith in Jesus as the Messiah and his baptized. A new chapter in the history of the church opens with this episode.

This easy evangelism is what many of us desire. The Spirit tells Philip where to go and to whom to talk. The eunuch asks Philip to teach him. He is reading from Isaiah 53, that great chapter on the suffering servant. He asks, "Who is the prophet speaking of?" Under those circumstances, even the most timid among us could be an evangelist.

> *Jesus himself takes the lead in evangelism.*

Evangelism is not always this easy, even in the rest of Acts. But in all of Acts, Jesus himself takes the lead in evangelism. He empowers his witnesses through his Spirit. He scatters and sends them. He gives them words to say. These early Christians are not experts on the strategies and techniques of evangelism, but rather experts on the heart of the good news—Jesus himself.

Reflection and Application

1. Are there certain groups we avoid in our outreach? Would we have targeted an Ethiopian eunuch?

2. What makes us less evangelistic than this early church? If an angel or the Spirit told us to go and preach, would we? What frightens us about evangelism?

Loving the Enemy (Acts 9:1-31)

In one case, Jesus takes a direct role in evangelism. It is Jesus himself who confronts Saul on the road to Damascus. Saul was so convinced that Jesus was a false Messiah and a dead Messiah, that he goes all the way to Damascus to persecute disciples. Then he hears the voice he least expects to hear, the voice of a risen, living Jesus.

Saul's life turns upside down (or rather, rightside up). No wonder he fasts and prays. He has killed those who follow the risen Jesus. He has persecuted the Messiah for whom he has longed all his life. Then, Ananias comes with good news. Jesus has chosen the great persecutor to be his great witness. Saul is healed and baptized—and immediately he begins to preach.

Saul also receives a dose of his own medicine. The great persecutor is himself now persecuted. He has to flee Damascus for his life. Coming to Jerusalem, this one who completely misunderstood the disciples is himself misunderstood. It is not until Barnabas stands up for him that the apostles accept Paul as a true follower of Jesus.

What power Jesus has! The power to end persecution, not by destroying the opposition, but by *converting* the opponent. What or who are the greatest opponents of Jesus today? Do we believe he has the power to overcome, perhaps even to convert them?

Reflection and Application

1. Why is Ananias reluctant to go to Saul? Is there someone you are reluctant to confront? How does Jesus help us overcome that reluctance?

2. Have you ever had your mind suddenly changed about something or someone? Can you imagine what Saul must have felt when he heard the voice of Jesus? Can we experience conversion as Paul did?

A Closer Look

1. What discourages you about the state of the church today? Does it seem the church is defeated? What in this chapter encourages you about the church?

2. Jesus showed love for Saul, one of his greatest enemies. What are some concrete ways we as individuals and as a church can show love to our enemies?

6

The Gospel is for All

Acts 9:32-12:24

Jesus Alive!

Christ died for all. That's the central teaching of the gospel. However, it takes the power of the living Lord to convince his disciples that the good news is truly for everyone. Jesus did not merely give his disciples his teaching during his earthly life and then leave them to interpret it for themselves. No, the living Jesus still works through situations and signs to move his disciples into a new and even frightening expansion of his ministry.

Good News to the Jews Outside Jerusalem (Acts 9:32-43)

Peter's brief trip to Samaria shakes him out of his "Jerusalem comfort" and makes him a missionary. In Lydda, he visits disciples scattered by the persecution. There he performs a great miracle, healing a paralyzed man. However, Peter makes it clear he is not healing the man—Jesus is. "Jesus Christ heals you" (Acts 9:34). In the same way that he healed a paralytic when he was present in the flesh (Luke 5:24), Jesus now heals through Peter. Again, Acts is the story of the continuing ministry of Jesus.

In Joppa, an even greater miracle occurs. Tabitha or Dorcas (we would call her "Gazelle") had spent her life in quiet Christian service. When she dies, the disciples send for Peter. He sends the mourners from the room, prays, and tells Tabitha to arise. She does! Where had Peter seen this miracle happen before? Remember that Jesus had taken him, along with James and John, into a dead girl's room, then told her to get up from her death bed (Luke 8:51-56). It is Jesus who continues to raise the dead.

Do we sometimes put too much emphasis on Peter and the apostles and not enough on Jesus, who works through them?

Reflection and Application

1. Do we sometimes put too much emphasis on Peter and the apostles and not enough on Jesus, who works through them? Do we have the tendency today to place too much emphasis on ministers and other leaders?

2. Does Jesus still have the power to heal and raise the dead? Does he do these things? If so, how?

Good News to Gentiles (Acts 10:1-11:18)

Although Jesus had told his disciples they would be witnesses "to the ends of the earth (Acts 1:8), it takes two visions to get Peter to the house of Cornelius. Cornelius is a Roman from a pagan background, but someone (perhaps the Jews in Caesarea) has introduced him to the true God. When praying to that God, he has a vision of an angel, directing him to send to Joppa for Peter.

The next day, Peter himself has a vision during prayer. A sheet with all kinds of animals is lowered before him and a voice tells him to kill and eat. Although hungry, Peter refuses, since some of these animals are unclean. The voice replies, "Do not call anything impure that God has made clean" (Acts 10:15). While he ponders the meaning of the vision, messengers from Cornelius arrive at his door. This time the Spirit directs Peter to go with them.

We know the rest of the story. Peter visits Cornelius and his family, tells them the story of Jesus, and witnesses the Spirit falling on them as he did upon the apostles. Astounded, Peter orders Cornelius to be baptized in the name of Jesus Christ.

This story is a turning point in Acts. The gospel now comes to the Gentiles. Although Peter had received criticism for eating with the uncircumcised, when he recounted his experience, the church in Jerusalem supported his actions.

But what is the point of the story? Why did God send an angel to Cornelius, not others? Because he was seeking after God. He prayed to God. What's more, he gave to those in need. It's not that Cornelius earned God's grace, but rather by his generosity he displayed the heart of God. The lesson Peter learns is "God does not show favoritism but accepts men from every nation who fear him and do what is right" (Acts 10:34-35).

Have we learned that lesson? Do we still think that God prefers a certain race or nationality? Does God speak English? With a Southern accent? Does he only recognize those who worship him in a church building with a particular name outside? No. God loves all who seek him. That is what it takes, not a particular religious pedigree or social lifestyle. God wants hearts who seek him. That is the lesson of Cornelius.

Reflection and Application

1. Do you think there are those around us who seek God, but do not know the gospel? Are our churches seeking them? Is God?

2. Do missionaries sent out by our churches sometimes get in trouble with the folks back home because they don't do things on the mission field the same way we do? What would Peter say in that situation? Does the church have to look the same in every culture? Why or why not?

A Church of Jews and Gentiles (Acts 11:19-30)

The action of Peter with Cornelius, and the approval of the Jerusalem church, leads us to the story of a larger Gentile mission. Note how the gospel spreads from country to country, from Jerusalem to Cyprus to Antioch, where Greeks along with Jews hear and believe it. The Antioch church is the first "mixed church" of Jews and Gentiles in Acts. That integration had to be upsetting to many who felt that, while Gentiles *could* become disciples (the Cornelius episode proves that), they should have their own separate churches.

A church shares what it has with those in need.

The experience of the Antioch church disproves this "separate but equal" view of the church. The Antioch church has both Jewish and Gentile members. It is an evangelistic and growing church because the Lord's hand is on it. A church shares what it has with those in need. In other words, this church is a model church, similar to the description of the Jerusalem church in Acts 2.

Besides this similarity in description, Barnabas is another tie to the Jerusalem church. Not only was he "a good man, full of the Holy Spirit and faith" (Acts 11:23), but he also was from Cyprus. Thus, the Jerusalem church sent a fellow countryman of those who had preached to the Gentiles to check on the Antioch church. What Barnabas saw so encouraged him that he went to look for someone to help him in the Antioch work. Going to Tarsus, he found Saul, brought him back to Antioch, and the two of them taught great numbers of people.

Here the disciples were first called "Christians." This naming has several implications. It shows that the Antioch disciples were numerous enough to have an identity and even a nickname in the community. It marks the entry of the church into the larger Roman world. The citizens of Antioch can no longer categorize the followers of Jesus as "Jews," since some are Greek-speaking Gentiles. Instead, they get a new name, "Christian."

Reflection and Application

1. Do we sometimes try to keep peace in the church by dividing into separate assemblies based on age, race, nationality, or even worship styles? Is this a good practice? What would they say about it in Antioch?

2. Should we continue to use the name "Christian," or does it have too much negative "baggage" in our world? How do you think the people of Antioch felt about the word?

Further Persecution (Acts 12:1-25)

While the gospel is spreading even to the Gentiles, the home church in Jerusalem faces more severe persecution. Herod Agrippa I (the grandson of Herod the Great, who persecuted Jesus) executes an apostle, James the brother of John. Herod then arrests Peter, intending to kill him after the Passover.

The church responds to this persecution the same way it did to earlier trials. It meets for prayer in the house of Mary, mother of John Mark. The church prays fervently for Peter's release. While they pray, Peter comes to the courtyard gate of the house! An angel has released him from his cell. When the servant girl reports his presence at the door, the church cannot believe it; they think it his angel or perhaps a ghost. Only after Peter continues to knock do they admit him to the house, hear his story, and praise God.

Two lessons from this story. Prayer is sometimes effective, even when those praying lack some faith. The disciples prayed for Peter's release—but could not believe Jesus would act so quickly. The second lesson is on the ways of Jesus. He works in *his* own way, not in ours. Sometimes, in times of persecution, he sends power and boldness (Acts 4:31). Sometimes, as with Stephen and James, he allows his servants even to die for him. Here, he immediately and miraculously delivers Peter from jail. The point is that God acts when we pray in the name of Jesus. He may not act exactly like we want him to, but he certainly hears and answers. He even punishes Herod with death for his persecution and his pride. Again, it is Jesus who is in control, not political authorities. The gospel spreads in spite of persecution.

> *God acts when we pray in the name of Jesus.*

Reflection and Application

1. Do we sometimes grow disappointed with God when he doesn't answer prayer our way? Should we? Does the immediacy of God's answers to prayer sometimes surprise us? Should it?

2. In what way do "authorities" (government, media, and public opinion) still oppose the gospel? Is Jesus still Lord over them?

A Closer Look

1. Why are we sometimes reluctant to reach out with the gospel to those different from us? Are our differences more severe than those between Jews and Gentiles? Of what are we afraid?

2. Prayer for the persecuted did not always keep them from death in the Book of Acts. Should this lack of rescue discourage us from praying? Why pray if God will not always deliver us?

7

Paul and Barnabas to the Gentiles

Acts 13:1-15:35

Jesus Alive!

The resurrected Jesus has all power. We see that power at work in his disciples. How do others react to the powerful Jesus? Some react with fear and obedience; some hear the message about the powerful Jesus; others worship the messengers, but later turn on them. A powerful, living Jesus frightens, comforts, and confounds.

The Gospel Again Confronts Sorcery (Acts 13:1-12)

How do we choose missionaries? Often we simply send anyone *willing* to go. Here the church is worshipping and fasting as the Spirit lets them know whom to send. How do we send out missionaries today? Often we send them with little thought or fanfare. Our fears of "ordination" and of giving ministers too much authority sometimes keeps us from any ceremony dedicating them to the Lord. Here, the Antioch leaders fast, pray, and lay their hands on Barnabas and Saul.

Accompanied by John Mark, these two missionaries sail to Cyprus (the home of Barnabas, Acts 4:36). There they face a Jewish false prophet and sorcerer named Elymas or Bar-Jesus ("son of Jesus or son of Joshua"). This strange character embodies the opposition of certain Jews to the gospel, the struggle of Jesus with the devil (see Luke 4:1-13), and the contest of the gospel with sorcery (see Acts 8:9-24).

It is Saul (from now on known as Paul) who takes the lead in opposing Elymas, striking him blind. Again, the question of power returns. Who has the power, Jesus through the Holy Spirit in Paul, or "Son of Jesus," this child of the devil? The answer is clear. The proconsul, who is also named Paul, comes to faith in Jesus because of the power he saw and the teaching he heard.

Reflection and Application

1. Should we send workers off with prayer, fasting, and laying on of hands? Was this practice only for the early church or is it an example we should follow? What was its purpose?

2. Is the devil still active today? Does Jesus still powerfully oppose him? How do we see that opposition at work? What does this passage teach concerning spiritual warfare?

Paul Proclaims the Good News (Acts 13:13-14:7)

The events in Cyprus are a turning point in this mission. Now instead of "Barnabas and Saul" (Acts 13:2), the group is "Paul and his companions" (Acts 13:13). It is Paul who speaks in the synagogue in Pisidian Antioch.

Paul's sermon is similar to earlier ones in Acts by Peter. Since this is the only lengthy record of Paul's preaching in Acts, we can assume that Luke intends it as typical.

Paul begins like Stephen, telling the story of God's redemption of Israel from slavery. He then turns to David and quickly gets to Jesus. Paul proclaims good news, that through the death and resurrection of Jesus, God's promises to his people come true. Forgiveness of sins and justification come to Jew and Gentile through Jesus.

The reaction to this message is positive, but cautious. Those in the synagogue ask to hear Paul again the next Sabbath. Some could not wait, but followed Paul and Barnabas around, asking questions.

The next Sabbath, a huge crowd gathers. How great, to see the gospel draw a crowd! But the popularity of Paul and Barnabas makes the synagogue leaders jealous (just as the leaders were jealous of Jesus and the apostles). Therefore, Paul and Barnabas turn to the Gentiles. The Gentiles of Antioch receive the gospel gladly, until the Jewish leaders stir up trouble for Paul with the leading citizens of the city. Shaking the dust off their feet, they move on to Iconium. However, this persecution does not discourage the church. The Holy Spirit fills the disciples with joy.

In Iconium, it's the same story. Initial success in the synagogue with both Jews and Gentiles is followed by opposition from the Jews who do not believe. This time the opposition threatens to turn violent. The missionaries hear of the plan and leave for Lystra.

Reflection and Application

1. Is popularity always good for the spread of the gospel? How does Jesus react to crowds in the gospels? Does God care about large numbers?

2. How should we react when some will not accept the good news of Jesus? When do we turn to others? Can we spend too much time with those who refuse to hear?

From "Gods" to Criminals (Acts 14:8-28)

What does it mean to "turn to the Gentiles?" Paul and Barnabas begin to find out when they confront the people of Lystra directly, without the aid of the synagogue. They heal a lame man (or rather Jesus heals him as he did a paralytic in Luke 5:17-26, and as he healed the lame man through Peter and John in Acts 3:1-10).

The reaction to the miracle is unexpected. This pagan crowd believes the gods have come down in human form, as many of their myths told. After all, only the gods can heal a lame man! They identify Barnabas as Zeus, the father of the gods, and Paul as Hermes, the messenger of the gods. They want to sacrifice to them as gods.

What could be more horrible for two faithful Jews than to be mistaken for gods? After all, the heart of the Jewish faith (and of Christianity) is the confession that there is one God. Barnabas and Paul barely manage to avoid their sacrifices by telling them about the one true God who made heaven and earth.

What happens next is one of the greatest turn-arounds in the Bible, similar to Jesus being proclaimed a king one day and being crucified as a blasphemer five days later. The unbelieving Jews come from Antioch and Iconium and convince these Gentiles that Paul and Barnabas are dangerous. They drag Paul from the city (just as he had once dragged disciples to jail) and stone him to death—at least they think he's dead. However, the disciples gather round him (in prayer?), and he gets up and goes back into the city.

The next day Paul and Barnabas leave Lystra and retrace their steps. Visiting the disciples they had made, they encourage them and appoint elders to lead them. Finally, they return to Antioch and report on their mission to the home church.

Reflection and Application

1. Do contemporary "pagans," even in America, sometimes confuse the gospel with their "gods?" Do we combine the "gods" of health, pleasure, wealth, and power with Christianity? What must we do to stop such misunderstanding?

2. What makes a crowd turn so fast against Jesus? Against Paul and Barnabas? Do people today quickly turn against Christians? Why?

The Gospel is for All? (Acts 15:1-35)

Why would anyone object to the preaching of the gospel? Why would anyone question the "rightness" of those wanting to be Christian? Perhaps for good reason. Not all who claim the name of Jesus are true disciples. However, there are also bad reasons for questioning the faith of others. Sometimes this distrust is out of fear, jealousy, or a misunderstanding of the gospel.

This time, perhaps all three are involved. Some think circumcision and keeping the law is required of both Jew and Gentile. Afraid of what might happen if they let "those people" into the church, and jealous of the success of Paul and Barnabas, certain Pharisees cause controversy and debate.

The discussion moves to Jerusalem. There the leaders of the church hear Peter again tell the story of his call to go to Cornelius. Barnabas and Paul (note the order of names now that they are back in Jerusalem) tell what God had done through them among the Gentiles. James, the most respected leader of the Jerusalem church, concludes, "we should not make it difficult for the Gentiles who are turning to God" (Acts 15:19).

The whole church agrees and sends a letter to the Gentile believers, placing the following requirements on them: stay away from meat sacrificed to idols, blood, and sexual immorality. The prohibition of sexual immorality is understandable, but aren't these food laws for Jews? Isn't the church doing exactly what James did *not* want it to do, placing unnecessary burdens on Gentile converts?

No. Not under the circumstances of these early believers. Later, Paul will say that eating meat sacrificed to idols is not wrong, unless it causes another believer to sin by going against conscience (1 Corinthians 10:14-33). So why the prohibition here? Because Jews could not eat with Gentiles who ate meat sacrificed to idols or meat that was not killed in a certain way that removed the blood. In other words, the Gentiles are asked to give up certain freedoms for the sake of table-fellowship.

The gospel is truly good news for all.

Paul, Barnabas, Judas Barsabbas, and Silas are sent with the letter to the Gentiles. They receive this letter not as a burden, but with joy. They are not burdened with the whole law, but asked only to do what is necessary for peace in the church. The gospel is truly good news for *all*.

Reflection and Application

1. What unnecessary difficulties do we sometimes place in the path of new converts? Why do we do so? What can we do to stop?

2. How should the church solve strong disagreements? Is there something we can learn from the examples in this chapter?

A Closer Look

1. Why is it so difficult to take the gospel into a different culture? Why do we tend to insist that those we convert do things exactly the way we did back home? Must every church look alike?

2. Why did certain Pharisees object to Gentile converts? Why did certain Pharisees object to Jesus eating with "sinners?" Do we object to certain evangelistic techniques? Should we? What can we do to avoid being like these Pharisees?

8

The Gospel Comes to Europe

Acts 15:36-18:22

Jesus Alive!

At his trial, Jesus confronted the Jewish rulers and the imperial might of Rome. Those forces conspired to put him to death on a cross. Here the living Jesus confronts them again. Many of his own people turn against him. Others believe. Again there are Romans who oppose the gospel, but many believe. Jesus gains the victory over unbelievers, not by force but by the good news of his love.

New Companions, New Direction (Acts 15:36-16:10)

Why can't we all just get along? What happens when Christians disagree? Paul and Barnabas sharply disagree over John Mark. Paul does not want to take him on this journey, since he deserted them on the first one (Acts 13:13). Barnabas, the one who gave Paul another chance, wants to do the same for John Mark. Although the disagreement is severe, they do not part as enemies but go their separate ways to preach the good news. Proclaiming God's love is more important than determining who is right or wrong.

> *Proclaiming God's love is more important than determining who is right or wrong.*

Paul takes Silas with him and soon they meet another companion, a young man named Timothy. Paul tells Timothy to be circumcised, although Paul had just finished fighting against the requirement of circumcision at the Jerusalem council. Is Paul inconsistent? No, for Timothy is technically a Jew since his mother is a Jewess. Paul never urged Jews to disobey the law; rather, he insisted Gentiles do not have to keep the Jewish ceremonies to be saved.

Paul, Silas, and Timothy find themselves on the coast at Troas. The Spirit will not allow them to go east or north. They had already preached in the south. Where were they to go? Paul gets the answer in a vision of a man of Macedonia calling for help. This turning point in the history of the church enables the gospel to go west to Europe. Even today, many consider Christianity a "western" (that is European and American) religion, although it began in the east and there are Christians worldwide.

1. When does disagreement get in the way of proclaiming the gospel? Do we care more about "being right" than we care about leading others to Jesus?

2. In Acts 16:7, the Holy Spirit is called "the Spirit of Jesus." Do we ever think of the Spirit as the presence of Jesus? Do we sometimes make too much of a separation between Jesus and the Spirit? How does the Spirit of Jesus lead us today?

Good News to a Roman Colony (Acts 16:11-40)

At Philippi, the gospel encounters a Roman colony. On the way to a place of prayer, Paul, Luke (note the "we"), and others proclaim the good news to a group of women including the remarkable Lydia. She sells purple cloth, runs a household, and is "a worshipper of God" (probably a Gentile influenced by Jewish worship). The Lord opens her heart, she responds along with her household, and all of them are baptized. She immediately extends hospitality to the missionaries.

Next, Paul and his companions face a slave girl with some kind of spirit (a demon?) that allows her to predict the future. Her owners had made money off her ability. Like the demons in the gospels who recognized Jesus, this slave girl recognizes him in the missionaries. Finally, Paul is annoyed enough to cast the spirit out of her in the name of Jesus. Again, as with Simon the sorcerer and Bar-Jesus, we have the theme of the power of Jesus over other spirits.

The result of this miracle is unexpected. The owners of the girl accuse Paul and Silas of disrupting a Roman city with Jewish customs. Paul knows what it's like to be persecuted by unbelieving Jews. This time he is thrown in prison for being a Jew! But even beating and imprisonment cannot stop the power of the gospel. After their miraculous release, Paul and Silas speak the word to the jailer and his family. They believe, are baptized, and (like Lydia) offer Paul and Silas hospitality.

> *The power of the living Jesus rules.*

However, the clash between Paul and the Roman authorities is not over. When the magistrates of the city send officers to release them from prison, Paul tells them he is a Roman citizen and his arrest was illegal. The magistrates personally come and politely request him and his companions to leave. Again the power of the living Jesus rules. He makes converts, casts out demons, releases from prison, and confounds the authorities.

Reflection and Application

1. What does it mean when it says God opened Lydia's heart to respond to Paul's message? Does conversion come through persuasion or through the work of God on the heart? What is the place of preaching?

2. Do those who spread the gospel today sometimes face cultural barriers and opposition? Why did these Romans oppose Paul? Why do some oppose missionaries today? How does American culture oppose the gospel?

Rejection and Acceptance from Jew and Greek (Acts 17:1-33)

Many Thessalonians, both Jew and Greek, respond to the gospel. The Jewish leaders there, out of jealousy, want to bring Paul and Silas to trial before the city assembly, but cannot find them. Note again the similarity between the trial of Jesus—jealousy, charges of troublemaking, and disloyalty to Caesar—and the charges against Paul and Silas. Jesus is still on trial before the authorities!

Escaping from Thessalonica, Paul and Silas find an even more receptive group at Berea—receptive until the Jewish leaders from Thessalonica come and stir up trouble for them. Because of this agitation, the church sends Paul to Athens alone.

In Athens, Paul faces Greek philosophy head-on. Asked to explain his teachings to a group of philosophers, he begins with their own religious experience, not with the Scriptures. He proclaims the God he worships *is* the unknown God they also worship in ignorance. From creation by the one God, he moves to God's desire for fellowship with humans to repentance and judgment as necessary for that fellowship. Judgment will be through Jesus, the man raised from the dead.

Talk of the resurrection turns most of the philosophers against Paul's message. However, a few men and women believe. Was Paul's evangelistic strategy at Athens successful? It's hard to say. More importantly, it was a strategy faithful to the gospel message.

Reflection and Application

1. Do some leaders today still reject Jesus and his message out of jealousy? Is it easy to surrender power to Jesus? Why or why not?

2. How should we approach contemporary "pagans" with the gospel? Should we start with the Bible or with their own experience? What approach do you think Paul would use today?

A Turn to the Gentiles at Corinth (Acts 18:1-22)

Paul meets Aquila and Priscilla, fellow tentmakers and fellow believers, at Corinth. Paul supported himself, at times, through tentmaking, but after Silas and Timothy come from Macedonia, perhaps bringing financial support with them, he devotes all his time to proclaiming the gospel to the Jews.

However, most in the synagogue (with the notable exception of Crispus) abusively reject the gospel. Paul then goes next door to preach to the Gentiles! Many believe and are baptized.

Opposition from the Jews continues. The Lord assures Paul in a vision that no one will harm him because the Lord "has many people in this city." The harm does not come, although the unbelieving Jews try unsuccessfully to get the ruler of the city on their side. The townspeople even turn on the new ruler of the synagogue, Sosthenes, and beat him up!

Paul decides to return to Antioch. He stops briefly in Ephesus, leaving Priscilla and Aquila there, then sails to Caesarea, and goes overland to Antioch. Thus ends what we generally call his second missionary journey, when the gospel comes to Europe and the heart of Roman and Greek culture.

Reflection and Application

1. Should missionaries support themselves through other vocations or is it best for them to be "full-time"? What can we learn from Paul's example?

2. What does the Lord mean when he says, "I have many people in this city?" Is he talking of those who will believe in the gospel? If Jesus knows ahead of time who will believe, does he predestine that faith?

A Closer Look

1. Considering the Christian companions of Paul in these chapters—Barnabas, John Mark, Silas, Timothy, Priscilla, and Aquila—reflect on your own "companions" in the faith. Who makes your faith stronger and helps you minister to others?

2. Can we completely understand how Jesus opens the heart of some and not others? What might this action of Jesus imply about the place of prayer in evangelism? Is Paul the great evangelist in Acts—or is Jesus? Does Jesus still evangelize?

9

The Gospel Meets Success and Opposition

Acts 18:23-20:38

Jesus Alive!

Paul is not Jesus. We may sometimes admire Paul too much. He is merely a man. But Jesus lived in Paul. Here we see how the living Jesus reacts to different situations through Paul. He is gentle but firm in helping those with inadequate understanding and experience of discipleship. He is a powerful healer and proclaimer. He is a hard worker for others and embodies his own teaching that it is better to give than to receive. We serve a risen, giving Lord.

Right on Jesus, Wrong on Baptism (Acts 18:23-19:7)

Apollos looks like the ideal Christian proclaimer. He knows the Scriptures and teaches correctly about Jesus with great fervor. His only problem is that he is "wrong on baptism," wrong in the sense that he knows only of the baptism of John the Baptist.

Notice how Priscilla and Aquila treat him. They do not publicly rebuke him in the synagogue as a false teacher. Instead they invite him to their home as a brother and teach him more accurately concerning baptism. Because of their gentle teaching, Apollos becomes a powerful missionary to Achaia.

The other part of the story involves Paul and twelve disciples. "Disciple" is the word used most often in Acts for followers of Jesus. Luke uses it synonymously with "Christian" (Acts 11:26); therefore, these men are Christians but they had never heard of the Holy Spirit! Such ignorance of the Spirit alerts Paul that something was not adequate about their baptism. Like Apollos (they may have heard the gospel from him before he knew it adequately), they have only received John's baptism. Paul tells them of baptism in the name of Jesus. They are baptized and receive the Holy Spirit.

What are we to make of these two related stories? We live in a very different age than Paul, an age where there are millions of people who love Jesus, who want to follow the Bible as closely as possible, but who have never heard that baptism is believer's immersion. These stories may help us learn how to treat them—not as false teachers, but as disciples who need someone to show them gently and adequately the way of the Lord.

Reflection and Application

1. Is our current religious situation similar to the experiences in this chapter? If so, what can we learn from the way Priscilla, Aquila, and Paul acted?

2. Can we call those today, who were baptized as infants, "disciples"? Can we call them "Christians"? Should we teach them about baptism as believer's immersion?

Teaching, Miracles, and a Riot (Acts 19:8-40)

The pattern of Paul's experience continues in Ephesus. He preaches in the synagogue, faces opposition, then moves to a Gentile location—the lecture hall of Tyrannus. God also does amazing miracles through Paul (note that language), healing those who touch even aprons (used in tentmaking) and handkerchiefs used by Paul. Just as Jesus healed by the hem of his garment, and healed through the shadow of Peter, he now heals and casts out demons through Paul.

Some Jewish exorcists try to use the name of Jesus (the name Paul used) to cast out demons. However, they dramatically learn that the name of Jesus is not magical, but must be claimed only by those who have faith in Jesus. The lesson comes when the demon beats them up! As a result of this episode, many believers confess their continuing practice of sorcery. They repent and burn their valuable magic books.

In Ephesus, the gospel becomes a victim of its own success. So many are turning to Jesus that the local tradesmen, who made their living off the worship of Artemis, find their business suffering. They start a riot against the Christians and seize two of Paul's companions (the disciples keep Paul out of the riot). It takes the city clerk to end the riot.

Reflection and Application

What are some ways the gospel challenges "business as usual" in our society?

1. Are people today guilty of using the name of Jesus as a means to get what they want? What about businesses that advertise they are Christian? What are other ways his name is misused?

2. Can you imagine Christianity making such a difference in your community that it would cause a riot? What are some ways the gospel challenges "business as usual" in our society?

A Farewell Address (Acts 20:1-38)

In a hurry to get to Jerusalem, Paul passes through Troas, breaking bread with the disciples there on the first day of the week. The unusual aspect of the meeting is the sleepiness of Eutychus, his fall to his death, and Paul raising him from the dead. The parallels to the resurrection of Jesus and his appearance to disciples in the breaking of bread (Luke 24:31) are striking. Again, it is the resurrected Jesus who appears to the church at the breaking of bread and who raises the dead in Christ.

Stopping at Miletus, near Ephesus, Paul calls for the elders of the Ephesian church to meet with him. Having spent three years working with that church, Paul's farewell address to these leaders is moving. He tells them he will not see them face to face again. Paul defends his ministry among them by reminders that he had proclaimed the whole will of God to them. They are to care for the flock in Paul's absence, feeding it with the words of Jesus and protecting it from the wolves of false teaching.

Paul ends by committing them to God and his word, the one who can give them holiness. He urges them to follow his example of giving and reminds them of the words of Jesus (words not found in the four gospels): "It is more blessed to give than to receive" (Acts 20:35). He ends by kneeling with them in prayer, with tears at his parting.

What can we learn about leadership from this speech? True Christian leaders are to be bold in their proclamation, genuine in their care for others, vigilant against false teaching, and generous in their giving. This pattern Jesus left them through Paul.

Reflection and Application

1. How do you picture Paul? Would he be tough to get along with? Was he too strict for contemporary tastes? Not warm and emotional? How does your picture square with the description of Paul in this section?

2. How does Paul describe false teachers in this section? How do you feel about the threat of false teaching? Has the church overplayed or understated that threat?

A Closer Look

1. We in Churches of Christ have typically claimed to be "Christians only, not the only Christians." If we are not the only Christians, how can we fellowship others and still stand firm for the truth in areas where we disagree? Does the Apollos story help at all here?

2. In what ways would you most want to be like Paul? What aspects of his life and personality would you least want to imitate? Is Paul our example in all things?

10

The Unstoppable Gospel

Acts 21:1-23-35

Jesus Alive!

Jesus was determined to go to Jerusalem. Knowing the danger he faced there, his disciples tried to convince him not to go. They failed. He went. Initially, those in Jerusalem greeted him warmly, as a conquering hero coming in the name of the Lord. But soon the Jewish leaders arrested him, turned him over to the Roman authorities, and had him crucified. We know the story.

In this section of Acts, it looks like the story will happen again. Jesus, in the person of Paul, is determined to go to Jerusalem. He is arrested and put on trial before the Jewish leaders and the Roman governor. Will there be another martyrdom like the one of which we read in the gospels? Will Jesus be crucified again in the person of Paul?

A Prediction of Trouble (21:1-26)

Hurrying toward Jerusalem, Paul makes a brief stop in Caesarea, staying with Philip the evangelist. The prophet Agabus comes from Jerusalem, takes Paul's belt, and binds his own hands and feet. Like prophets of old (Ezekiel, for example), Agabus dramatically reveals the will of God. The Holy Spirit says the Jewish leaders in Jerusalem will bind Paul and hand him over to the Gentiles.

"Bind and hand over to the Gentiles." Where have we heard that before? Wasn't Jesus himself bound and handed to the Gentiles? Didn't the disciples plead with Jesus (as other disciples now plead with Paul) to avoid Jerusalem? But both Jesus and Paul are determined to go. Paul says he is ready to die in Jerusalem for the name of the Lord Jesus.

So Paul goes to Jerusalem. He receives a warm welcome from James and the other leaders. He reports to them what God has done through him among the Gentiles. These leaders have a minor request to Paul. Some are still spreading vicious rumors about Paul, rumors that he teaches Jews to break the Law of Moses. To show that is not the case, Paul agrees to join four Jews in fulfilling a vow they had made. He will go to the temple and sacrifice with them.

Reflection and Application

> *How do we know if we are following the voice of God or our own inclinations?*

1. Is Paul too bold? Should he have listened to the warning from the Holy Spirit and the pleading of his brothers in Christ? Or is his journey to Jerusalem the will of God? How do we know if we are following the voice of God or our own inclinations?

2. Is Paul inconsistent in going to the temple to sacrifice? Does Paul think he is saved by temple sacrifices? If not, why did he go?

Arrest in the Temple (Acts 21:27-40)

Some Jews from Asia see Paul in the temple and assume he had brought Gentiles into the temple area forbidden to them. They accuse Paul of speaking against the law and the temple (the same charges made against Jesus). A riot ensues, and the crowd beats Paul, intending to kill him. The Roman commander charged with keeping the peace in the temple area brings his troops and arrests Paul, although in the confusion he cannot learn what Paul had done.

On the way to the barracks, Paul startles the commander by speaking in Greek and asking to address the crowd. The commander agrees. Paul makes his defense to this mob in Aramaic (a surprise to some of them who may have thought him a Gentile). His defense is his conversion story. The crowd seems to listen, while Paul tells of persecuting Christians, of the vision near Damascus, and of his conversion. He loses the crowd when he tells them Jesus has sent him to the Gentiles. The crowd again begins to riot.

The commander takes Paul to the barracks, intending to "question" him in the typical way, by flogging him. Paul then tells the commander that he is a Roman citizen. The commander is both impressed and afraid. He has illegally (although unknowingly) arrested a Roman citizen.

This is more than an adventure story; it is the story of Jesus continued. Just as Jesus was rejected in Jerusalem, so now Paul's testimony about Jesus is rejected. Paul faces the same false charges and the same forces Jesus faced.

Reflection and Application

1. Did Paul teach against the law and the temple? Did Jesus? Are we under the law? Do we worship at the temple? Didn't Jesus do away with both? If so, are the charges against Jesus and Paul true? Or do we still have a law and temple from God?

2. After Paul's conversion, Jesus sent him away from Jerusalem (Acts 22:18). Why did Paul not want to leave then? Does this reluctance explain Paul's determination to be a witness in Jerusalem now?

Trial Before the Sanhedrin (Acts 22:30-23:35)

The commander places Paul before the Sanhedrin, allowing it to make some charge against him. Paul begins by proclaiming his innocence, which gets him a sock in the mouth by orders of the high priest Ananias (the same high priest at the trial of Jesus). Paul calls the high priest a whitewashed wall (as Jesus called the Pharisees whitewashed tombs). Accused of insulting the high priest, Paul (perhaps sarcastically) says he didn't know Ananias was the high priest; in other words, Ananias sure didn't act the way a high priest should!

Instead of explaining his actions in the temple, Paul calls himself a Pharisee and says he is on trial because he believes in the resurrection. Of course, Paul is on trial *because* of the resurrection, that is, the resurrection of Jesus. His statement turns the Pharisees (who believe in resurrection) against the Sadducees (who do not). A divided Sanhedrin can reach no decision about Paul.

Where is Jesus throughout Paul's ordeal? With him every step of the way. He stands beside him, encourages him, and tells him he will be a witness in Rome. Jesus works through Paul's nephew to inform the Roman commander that there is a plot among over forty Jews to kill Paul. The commander finally gets Paul out of his hair by sending him under guard to Felix, the Roman governor at Caesarea. With him he sends a letter explaining how he had "rescued" the Roman citizen Paul from a Jewish riot.

Jesus again stands before the Sanhedrin. He again will stand before a Roman governor. This time he stands in the person of Paul. Although Paul is willing to die for Jesus in Jerusalem, Jesus has other plans. He wills for Paul to witness in Rome.

Reflection and Application

1. What was the church doing while Paul was in custody? Earlier they prayed for Peter in jail. Have they abandoned Paul? Has Jesus abandoned him? Do we stand with those falsely accused, or is it easier to distance ourselves from them?

2. When accused of speaking against the high priest, Paul quotes Scripture (Acts 23:5), although he is on trial for speaking against the Law. Have you ever been accused of being "unscriptural" when you were trying your best to follow the Bible? Are we sometimes like the Sanhedrin, making false accusations against fellow Christians?

A Closer Look

1. Paul is not willing to avoid trouble for the sake of Jesus. Do we sometimes go too much out of our way to avoid offending others in church or in the world? When should we confront others, as Paul did the high priest?

2. Jesus gives powerful words to Paul: “Take courage” (Acts 23:11). When do you most need to hear those words? How often do you say them to others? What is the source of our courage as Christians?

11

The Gospel Before Kings

Acts 24:1-26:32

Jesus Alive!

Jesus is amazingly silent in Luke's account of his trials before the Sanhedrin and before Pilate. When asked by the Jewish council if he is Son of God, he answers, "Yes" (Luke 22:70). When asked by Pilate if he is king of the Jews, he again answers, "Yes" (Luke 23:3). Here in Acts, Jesus again has stood before the Sanhedrin and now stands before Roman governors and kings in the person of Paul. It's as if Jesus is saving his words to put them later in the mouth of Paul. These trials are not merely occasions for Paul to defend himself, but opportunities for him to defend the resurrection of Jesus. Paul makes it clear that Jesus—not Felix, Festus, Agrippa, or even Caesar—is truly Lord.

Lawyers and Politicians (Acts 24:1-23)

Ananias the high priest, accompanied by a slick Roman lawyer named Tertullus, comes to Caesarea to accuse Paul. Reading the lengthy praise Tertullus offers to governor Felix makes one feel almost oily. To think the Jews would view a Roman governor with gratitude is beyond imagination. The charges made against Paul are that he is a troublemaker who tried to desecrate the temple.

Paul begins his defense, not with flattery, but with a statement of fact. Felix has ruled for years and should know the Jewish situation. Paul briefly refutes the charges, then moves to a larger defense of the gospel. He argues two things. One, Paul and others of "the Way" are completely loyal to the Law and Prophets. Paul did not see Christianity as a new religion that was a threat to Judaism; instead, he saw himself proclaiming Jesus as the true hope of Israel. Two, Paul speaks often of the resurrection. He defends not only a general resurrection of the dead, but also specifically the resurrection of Jesus.

Felix responds by basically doing nothing. He waits for the Roman commander to come from Jerusalem and testify. In the meantime, he keeps Paul under guard but allows his friends to visit and care for him.

Reflection and Application

1. Do we sometimes make too great a distinction between Judaism and Christianity? How Jewish is Christianity? Are not even Gentiles now part of the true Israel through Christ? What attitude should we have toward Jews today?

2. Do we act as if the resurrection were really at the heart of our faith? How often do we talk about the resurrection? How does it change how we live each day?

An Indecisive Governor (Acts 24:24-27)

At first, it looks like Felix is ignoring Paul's case. However, we find, accompanied by his wife Drusilla, Felix sends for Paul and listens to him. What makes this request significant is that Felix is not the first husband of Drusilla. According to the Jewish historian Josephus, Felix had stolen her away from her first husband and married her—contrary to the Law of Moses.

Josephus' account puts Paul's words to Felix and Drusilla in a different light. What do you say to a powerful governor who holds your life in his hands? Do you merely flatter (as lawyer Tertullus had done), or do you confront him with his behavior? Paul speaks of "righteousness, self-control, and the judgment to come." The reaction of Felix shows he understands that Paul is speaking directly to his marriage situation. Felix is afraid. Unfortunately, that fear does not move Felix to repentance but to rejection; he dismisses Paul until he finds it more convenient to hear him.

Amazingly, Felix does send for Paul again, even often. No doubt, Paul speaks again of righteousness, self-control, and judgment. Is Felix close to accepting the good news of Jesus? No. He wants not salvation, but a bribe. He does not give justice to Paul, but keeps him in prison for two long years.

Reflection and Application

> *Are we afraid to confront powerful people with the consequences of their actions?*

1. Are we afraid to confront powerful people with the consequences of their actions? Would you correct an immoral action of your boss if it cost you a promotion or your job? What excuses do we give for avoiding such confrontations? Do we have more to lose than Paul?

2. Are there similarities between Felix and Pilate? What weaknesses do they share? What are the consequences of their inaction?

Another Governor and another Herod (Acts 25:1-26:32)

The danger to Paul increases with the arrival of a new governor, Festus. While Felix had dithered on Paul's case, Festus seems determined to please the Jewish leaders by sending Paul back to Jerusalem. Since Paul had been sent to Caesarea under guard to protect him from a murder plot by the unbelieving Jews, his return to Jerusalem equals a death sentence. Since Jesus had already told Paul he would be a witness in Rome (Acts 23:11), Paul appeals to Caesar.

While waiting to send Paul to Rome, a visiting king comes and wants to hear Paul. His name is Agrippa, but his family name is Herod. So far, the gospel had not fared well under Herods. Herod the Great opposed Jesus at his birth; his son, Herod Antipas, beheaded John the Baptist and ridiculed Jesus at his trial; Herod Agrippa I (the father of this Agrippa) killed James the brother of John and imprisoned Peter (Acts 12). Now Paul stands before yet another Herod.

Paul does not defend himself against the specific charges laid against him by the Jewish leaders in Jerusalem. Instead, he defends his entire life and ministry. Again, he tells his life story. He has always hoped in the promises of God. That hope led him to oppose the name of Jesus, until he heard Jesus on the road to Damascus. Afterward, he was obedient to that vision and to the true hope of Israel. He proclaims only what Moses said would happen—that the Messiah would suffer and be raised from the dead. Paul's mission is not against the Jews but for them and Gentiles, too.

At that point of the story, Festus interrupts and calls Paul "insane." The resurrection is a stumbling block to this educated Roman governor. Paul then appeals to Agrippa's knowledge of these matters. Agrippa's reply is ambiguous; some older translations have him saying he is almost persuaded to be a Christian. More likely, his words are cynical, "Do you think you can convince me so quickly?" Paul is willing to take as much time as it takes to convince this latest Herod.

Seen on this level, Paul's defense is successful. Both governor and king agree Paul is innocent, although they can do nothing for him since he has appealed to Caesar. On another level, however, the gospel falls on deaf ears. These rulers do not hear what Paul wants them to hear most—that the resurrected Jesus offers them light and life.

Reflection and Application

1. In this account, Paul says Jesus at Damascus told him "It is hard to kick against the goads," implying Jesus was guiding (and goading) Paul's life before his conversion. Could Jesus be at work today even in the greatest enemies of Christianity? Would it change our attitude if we thought Jesus were goading those who oppose our faith?

2. Is Paul foolish to think he can convince Felix, Festus, and Agrippa of the gospel? Is he naïve or does he have more faith than we do?

A Closer Look

1. Why do you think Jesus is so quiet at his trials, while Paul talks so much? How are their circumstances different? Is there a time for us to be quiet in the face of persecution? A time to speak up?

2. Who has genuine power, political rulers or Jesus? How does that power affect the way we live? Do Christians make good Americans (or Germans or Japanese or Nigerians)?

12

THE GOSPEL AT THE HEART OF THE EMPIRE

ACTS 27:1-28:31

Jesus Alive!

If Acts really is a continuation of the gospel story, then what has Jesus done in this book? The resurrected Jesus appears to the apostles and commands them to wait in Jerusalem for power. Jesus sends the Spirit at Pentecost. He promises salvation and the Spirit to all baptized in his name. He encourages the persecuted, punishes the hypocrites, and maintains the unity of the church. He continues to heal the sick and cast out demons. He works through missionaries to spread his good news to Samaritans, Ethiopians, Italians, and throughout the Roman world. He turns the greatest persecutor into the greatest proclaimer. Here he goes with him to Rome to tell the good news at the very heart of the empire. Acts is the story of a living, active Jesus.

Shipwreck (Acts 27:1-44)

Luke gives a lengthy account of Paul's journey from Caesarea to Rome, a journey interrupted by a shipwreck at Malta. The most significant aspect of the journey is the way Jesus works through Paul to accomplish his purposes. Paul acts as a prophet, predicting disaster but being ignored as most prophets were (Acts 27:10-11). Later, an angel assures Paul that he will appear safely before Caesar and all on board with him would be spared (Acts 27:21-26). Paul stops a plot by the sailors to abandon the ship and urges all aboard to eat something to maintain their strength (Acts 27:30-38). In gratitude for his guidance, the centurion in charge prevents the soldiers from killing Paul and the other prisoners.

> *The most significant aspect of the journey is the way Jesus works through Paul to accomplish his purposes.*

Again, this is more than one's typical action and adventure story; this is an adventure into the power of God in Christ. Paul is in charge of the sea voyage, not the centurion nor the captain of the ship. Better put, Jesus is overseeing the voyage so Paul can be a witness in Rome.

Reflection and Application

1. Jesus chooses a roundabout way (and a dangerous one) to get Paul to Rome. Why? Does Jesus always work the way we expect him to in our lives? Give examples from your own life when God answered your prayers in unexpected ways.

2. Do you think the sailors and the soldiers on the ship would have told the story of the shipwreck the way Luke told it here? Can the hand of God only be seen by faith? Is it right to interpret events as acts of Jesus? How do we know when he is at work?

Snakebite (Acts 28:1-16)

Shipwrecked in Malta, Paul and the others encounter amazing kindness from the islanders. However, their attitude toward Paul changes when a deadly viper bites his hand. Knowing he is a prisoner, they assume he must be a terrible murderer and the "gods" are justly punishing him.

When Paul shows no ill effect from the bite, they completely change their mind and think him a god! This reaction is the reverse situation of Paul and Barnabas at Lystra, where the people first think them gods and later try to stone Paul to death (Acts 14:8-20). Paul later heals many on the island, including the father of the chief official.

After three months, they sail again to Italy and go overland to Rome. On the way, Christians from Rome come to greet Paul. Somehow, word of his arrival had preceded him. In Rome, although Paul has a guard, he is given limited freedom.

Reflection and Application

1. Are contemporary people less superstitious than those in ancient Malta? Do we still judge someone's standing before God based on his or her good or bad fortune? Do bad things only happen to bad people or good things to good?

2. Paul is encouraged by the Christians that come from Rome to greet him. What are some ways we can encourage those in need? How does Jesus work through others to strengthen us? How does he work through us for them?

The End? (Acts 28:17-30)

Paul's actions in Rome mirror his consistent missionary practices. He goes to the Jews first, calling the leaders in Rome to meet with him. He briefly explains his innocence of the charges against him, but spends most of his time trying "to convince them about Jesus from the law of Moses and the Prophets" (Acts 28:23). As in the rest of his missions, some Jews believe—but many do not. Therefore, he turns to the Gentiles with the message of God's salvation.

> *Acts is the story of the actions of the resurrected Christ.*

For two years, Paul speaks freely of the gospel to anyone who will listen. Luke ends Acts abruptly with Paul still in prison in Rome, indeed a strange place to end if we understand this book as the acts of the apostles. If it's about the apostles, why doesn't it tell us the *end* of their story?

However, if we understand Acts as a fifth gospel (or better, part two of Luke's Gospel), then the ending makes perfect sense. The book is not primarily about Paul, Peter, nor any apostle. Rather, Acts is the story of the actions of the resurrected Christ himself. Jesus sails with Paul, delivers him from shipwreck and snakebite, and allows him boldly to proclaim the gospel in Rome. No wonder the theme of the last verse of Acts is the Lord Jesus Christ (Acts 28:31). May that be the theme of the church today!

Reflection and Application

1. Why does Paul always begin with the Jews if they always reject the message? Can we know who will be receptive to the gospel before we proclaim it? How do we know when we are wasting time with those who will not hear?

2. Does the ending of Acts seem abrupt to you? How would you end the story? Why does Luke end it here? What does that tell us about Luke's purposes in writing?

A Closer Look

1. Some look to Acts to find a pattern for the church. Is there a pattern here? Is Jesus the pattern? In what way?

2. Is the experience of Jesus found in Acts meant only for the church back then? Is Jesus as active in the world now as then? If not, why not? If so, how do we see his hand at work? If you were writing the "Acts of Your Congregation," would it read like the Book of Acts?

CPSIA information can be obtained
at www.ICGtesting.com
Printed in the USA
LVHW041951110920
665558LV00003B/267

9 780891 122395